# BASEBALL LEGENDS

Hank Aaron
Grover Cleveland Alexander
Ernie Banks
Johnny Bench
Yogi Berra
Roy Campanella
Roberto Clemente
Ty Cobb
Dizzy Dean
Joe DiMaggio
Bob Feller
Jimmie Foxx
Lou Gehrig
Bob Gibson
Rogers Hornsby
Walter Johnson
Sandy Koufax
Mickey Mantle
Christy Mathewson
Willie Mays
Stan Musial
Satchel Paige
Brooks Robinson
Frank Robinson
Jackie Robinson
Babe Ruth
Duke Snider
Warren Spahn
Willie Stargell
Honus Wagner
Ted Williams
Carl Yastrzemski
Cy Young

CHELSEA HOUSE PUBLISHERS

BASEBALL LEGENDS

# BROOKS ROBINSON

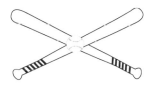

*Rick Wolff*

*Introduction by*
*Jim Murray*

*Senior Consultant*
*Earl Weaver*

## CHELSEA HOUSE PUBLISHERS
*New York • Philadelphia*

Produced by James Charlton Associates
New York, New York.

Designed by Hudson Studio
Ossining, New York.

Typesetting by LinoGraphics
New York, New York.

Picture research by Jennie McGregor
Cover illustration by Dan O'Leary

3 5 7 9 8 6 4

Library of Congress Cataloging-in-Publication Data

Wolff, Rick,
    Brooks Robinson / Rick Wolff ; introduction by Jim Murray.
        p. cm.—(Baseball legends)
    Includes bibliographical references.
    Summary: A biography of the Oriole third baseman whose
lifetime fielding average is tops among third baseman in major league
history.
    ISBN 0-7910-1186-0.
    ISBN 0-7910-1220-4 (pbk.)
    1. Robinson, Brooks, 1937- —Juvenile literature. 2. Baseball
players—United States—Biography—Juvenile literature.
[1. Robinson, Brooks, 1937- . 2. Baseball players.] I. Title.
II. Series.
    GV865.R58W65 1991
    796.357'092—dc20
[B]
                    90-31321
                        CIP
                        AC

# CONTENTS

# WHAT MAKES A STAR

*Jim Murray*

No one has ever been able to explain to me the mysterious alchemy that makes one man a .350 hitter and another player, more or less identical in physical makeup, hard put to hit .200. You look at an Al Kaline, who played with the Detroit Tigers from 1953 to 1974. He was pale, stringy, almost poetic-looking. He always seemed to be struggling against a bad case of mononucleosis. But with a bat in his hands, he was King Kong. During his career, he hit 399 home runs, rapped out 3,007 hits, and compiled a .297 batting average.

Form isn't the reason. The first time anybody saw Roberto Clemente step into the batter's box for the Pittsburgh Pirates, the best guess was that Clemente would be back in Double A ball in a week. He had one foot in the bucket and held his bat at an awkward angle—he looked as though he couldn't hit an outside pitch. A lot of other ballplayers may have had a better-looking stance. Yet they never led the National League in hitting in four different years, the way Clemente did.

Not every ballplayer is born with the ability to hit a curveball. Nor is exceptional hand-eye coordination the key to heavy hitting. Big-league locker rooms are filled with players who have all the attributes, save one: discipline. Every baseball man can tell you a story about a pitcher who throws a ball faster than anyone has ever seen, but who has no control on or *off* the field.

The Hall of Fame is full of people who transformed themselves into great ballplayers by working at the sport, by studying the game, and making sacrifices. They're overachievers—and winners. If you want to find them, just watch the World Series. Or simply read about New York Yankee great Lou Gehrig; Ted Williams, "the Splendid Splinter" of the Boston Red Sox; or the Dodgers' strikeout king Sandy Koufax.

A pitcher *should* be able to win a lot of ballgames with a 98-miles-per-hour fastball. But what about the pitcher who wins 20 games a year with a fastball so slow that you can catch it with your teeth? Bob Feller of the Cleveland Indians got into the Hall of Fame with a blazing fastball that glowed in the dark. National League star Grover Cleveland Alexander got there with a pitch that took considerably longer to reach the plate; but when it did arrive, the pitch was exactly where Alexander wanted it to be—and the last place the batter expected it to be.

There are probably more players with exceptional ability who didn't make it to the major leagues than there are who did. A number of great hitters, bored with fielding practice, had to be dropped from their team because their home-run production didn't make up for their lapses in the field. And then there are players like Brooks Robinson of the Baltimore Orioles, who made himself into a human vacuum cleaner at third base because he knew that working hard to become an expert fielder would win him a job in the big leagues.

A star is not something that flashes through the sky. That's a comet. Or a meteor. A star is something you can steer ships by. It stays in place and gives off a steady glow; it is fixed, permanent. A star works at being a star.

And that's how you tell a star in baseball. He shows up day after day and takes pride in how brightly he shines. He's Willie Mays running so hard his hat keeps falling off; Ty Cobb sliding to stretch a single into a double; Lou Gehrig, after being fooled in his first two at-bats, belting the next pitch off the light tower because he's taken the time to study the pitcher. Stars never take themselves for granted. That's why they're stars.

# FROM SERIES GOAT TO SERIES HERO

There were 51,531 fans crammed into Cincinnati's Riverfront Stadium as the Reds and Baltimore Orioles faced each other for game 1 of the 1970 World Series. As he stood on the field waiting to make his first play of the day, Baltimore third baseman Brooks Robinson felt 51,531 pairs of eyes focused right on him.

Robinson had good reason to feel self-conscious. Precisely one year earlier he had not played well in the 1969 Series against the New York Mets. The Orioles were a powerful ballclub, and their fans had fully expected them to sweep past the young Mets. But New York's Tom Seaver, Jerry Koosman, Ron Swoboda, and Al Weis had different plans: they derailed the Orioles and became known as the "Miracle Mets"—and the world champions.

The Orioles hit just .146 against New York pitching. Robinson had played particularly poorly

*Robinson robs Johnny Bench of a hit in game 3 of the 1970 World Series.*

against the Mets, getting just 1 hit in 19 at-bats—a measly single. That figured out to be a batting average of .053, to this day still one of the all-time worst offensive performances in a World Series.

But that was last year. Now the Orioles were taking on the mighty Cincinnati Reds, an all-star team led by Johnny Bench, Pete Rose, and Tony Perez. Robinson had not forgotten the miserable Series he had had in 1969 and he was determined to make up for it with a much better 1970 effort.

Robinson's first chance came in the bottom of the second inning. Woody Woodward, the Cincinnati shortstop, bounced an easy high-hopper down to him at third. Robinson came in on the ball, gloved it cleanly, and then fired what he thought would be a routine out to the big Baltimore first baseman, Boog Powell. But his throw sailed away from Powell, pulling his foot

*In game 4, Brooks hit safely his first three times at bat, but the Orioles lost 6-5. The loss stopped a winning streak of 17 games: 11 at the end of the regular season, 3 in the LCS, and the first 3 in the World Series.*

off the base. Woodward was safe at first, and Brooks Robinson, on his first play in the 1970 World Series, was charged with an error.

Robinson could not help wondering: Was this to be another nightmare of a World Series? A World Series just like the last one?

But Robinson need not have worried. That throwing error was hardly a sample of things to come. After his one fielding miscue, the Baltimore third baseman went on to put together one of the finest demonstrations of defensive baseball ever seen in a World Series. And when he was not robbing the Reds of hits in the field, Robinson was at the plate, supplying plenty of firepower.

The Reds jumped off to a 3-0 lead in game 1, but the Orioles came back with three runs of their own to tie it up. Then in the seventh inning, Brooks Robinson came up with the bases empty to face the Cincinnati starter, Gary Nolan. Nolan tried to throw a fast ball by Robinson, but with one swing he made up for his first-inning error. The ball landed deep in the stands at the new Riverfront Stadium and gave the Orioles the 4-3 win. By the time the fall classic came to an end, the Baltimore Orioles had defeated the Cincinnati Reds, 4 games to 1, and had been crowned world champs. Along the way, Robinson had batted .429 with 2 home runs, 2 doubles, and 6 runs batted in. Defensively, after that first error, he went on to handle 23 consecutive chances flawlessly, and many of them brilliantly.

For his heroic efforts with both bat and glove, Brooks Robinson was named the 1970 World Series Most Valuable Player. It was one of the most remarkable turnarounds in Series history.

# 2

# THE BIG LEAGUER FROM LITTLE ROCK

*Brooks (standing, far left) with his teammates on the 1949 Little Rock Midget League Champions.*

Brooks Robinson was born in Little Rock, Arkansas, on May 18, 1937. His full given name was Brooks Calbert Robinson, Jr., but his parents called him Buddy.

Brooks's grandfather had been the police chief of Little Rock, and his dad was a fireman. Brooks grew up in a part of town called Pulaski Heights, where his father first taught him and his younger brother, Gary, how to play baseball. Brooks Sr. had once played minor-league ball for the Little Rock Travelers, and he passed his love for the game on to his sons.

As a boy, Brooks loved to practice the game. If he was not in school or asleep, he could almost surely be found on the sandlot baseball field. All of his friends played as well, but on the rare occasions when he could not find anyone to play with, the youngster would go off on his own and practice his batting swing by hitting rocks with a sawed-off broom handle. Brooks would do this for hours, sometimes stopping only when the broom handle finally broke.

In 1948, when he was 11 years old, Brooks

*Main Street in Little Rock, Arkansas, in the late 1930s when Brooks was growing up.*

joined the Little Rock Midget League. In addition to pitching, he played the infield, and even then it was apparent to all observers that Brooks was exceptionally gifted at fielding grounders. Whereas lots of other kids would shy away from the hard-hit low balls, Brooks fearlessly moved in to make the plays.

The first year in the Midget League, Brooks's team won the Little Rock championship. And the following year, when Brooks was 12 years old, the same team went on to become state champions.

By then, Brooks could see that all his practice was beginning to pay off. In fact, he discovered that practice was a key to success in other areas of life as well as in baseball. One day, for example, he entered a bubblegum-blowing contest. The boy who produced the biggest bubble would win a new bicycle.

Brooks practiced as hard as he could, and on the day of the contest, he ended up blowing a bubble that was almost one foot across. Not

surprisingly, Brooks rode off on the shiny new bike.

But Brooks did not have much time for cycling. He was too busy playing ball. One afternoon, when he was still around 11 or 12 years old, Brooks was walking down the street looking for some friends to play with when he heard the sounds of a basketball game going on. He followed the pounding of the ball on the pavement to a fenced-in playground and stopped to check out the action. Only then did he discover that the boys who were playing were unable to hear or say anything, and that the playground belonged to the local school for the deaf.

Brooks was a bit uncomfortable at first; after all, he had never met any deaf boys before. So he just sat and watched. But then one of the players had to leave to go home, and in order to keep the sides even, the other boys waved Brooks onto the court.

Brooks could not talk to his new teammates

*Brooks Robinson in 1971, still blowing champion bubbles.*

because he did not know sign language. But soon after he started playing, they realized that it did not matter. He had no problem communicating with the other kids. As it turned out, they all "spoke" the same language—the language of basketball.

That night, when Brooks told his mother about his unusual experience, she smiled and reminded him that "Most of us are afraid of what we don't know." From that day on, Brooks found himself constantly going down to the school for the deaf to play basketball with his new friends, and eventually he even started to learn sign language as well.

But as much as Brooks enjoyed basketball and baseball, he could not play all the time. He had many responsibilities while growing up. In addition to his chores at home, he also worked

as a newspaper boy, delivering the Arkansas *Gazette* around his neighborhood. Each morning before sunrise, he would get up and run his paper route, earning $25 a month.

Brooks found the work tedious, but there was one stop in particular that made his job worthwhile. That was the home of Bill Dickey, a former New York Yankee catcher who had been a teammate of Babe Ruth and Lou Gehrig. A true star himself, Dickey would soon be elected to the Hall of Fame.

By this time, Brooks Robinson already knew exactly what he wanted to do when he grew up. He had spent an ample portion of his life listening to games of his favorite team, the St. Louis Cardinals, on his family radio, and he dreamed of one day playing in the major leagues.

In fact, when he was assigned to write an essay in class, the eighth-grader handed in a composition entitled "Why I Want to Play Professional Baseball." Brooks listed a number of reasons for his choice, including: "The hours are good and ballplayers are paid very well." He also explained why he felt particularly suited for such a difficult profession: "I'm not easily discouraged."

As Brooks summed it up: "If I make the major leagues, the one thing I want to do is play for the St. Louis Cardinals. What I like to do best is play third base or pitch. When you pitch you have a better chance to make it to the majors because baseball teams carry seven or eight pitchers while they carry only two players for each base."

Although Brooks was well aware that only a handful of players ever got that chance to sign a professional contract, and even fewer ever made it to the major leagues, he continued to dream

*Brooks Robinson and his wife Connie revisit Little Rock Central High School in 1966.*

about a big-league career. One thing he knew for sure—he did not want to be a fireman like his dad. Having spent a good deal of time in the firehouse, Brooks knew the dangers of a firefighter's life. He had seen all the scars on his dad's body from various burns.

During his junior high school days, word began to spread around the area that young Brooks Robinson was turning into a pretty good athlete. His friends even convinced him to play on the school football team. Brooks agreed, was named quarterback, and promptly led the team to an undefeated season and the Arkansas state junior high school championship.

One year of football was enough for Brooks, however. He was not about to take a chance on getting hurt playing football because that might ruin his chances of signing a pro baseball contract. But Brooks knew he still had a long way to go—and some obstacles to overcome along the road. For starters, his high school did not even have a baseball team!

Determined to play, Brooks ended up joining the local American Legion baseball team, the Doughboys. It turned out to be a good move. The Doughboys won the state championship three of the four years Brooks played with them.

But baseball was not the only game in town. During the winters Brooks stayed in shape by playing on the high school basketball team. Brooks was doing more than staying in shape; in his junior year at Little Rock High School, he was named to the all-state team.

Throughout these terrific teen years Brooks never lost sight of his big-league dreams. But as he got older and came up against other talented players, he could not help realizing that as good as he was, some of his abilities were limited. For example, Brooks was an outstanding fielder and a terrific hitter as well. But even though he grew to be tall and lanky, he was never blessed with outstanding running speed or, for that matter, a particularly strong throwing arm. If he was ever going to get a shot at the majors, he would have to keep working at his skills and develop every bit of his potential. And that was exactly what he set out to do.

# 3

# BROOKS'S BIG DECISION

**B**rooks Robinson graduated from Little Rock High School on May 27, 1955. But while most of his buddies spent that special night celebrating, Brooks went home relatively early. He knew he would be called upon to make some important decisions during the next few days, and he wanted to be well-rested and clear-headed.

The first decision involved choosing between the two sports he liked the most: basketball and baseball. As a basketball player, his outstanding high school performances caught the attention of several college coaches. One of them, from the University of Arkansas, had already offered Brooks a full scholarship if he would agree to play basketball there.

It was a most tempting offer. Not only would Brooks be able to play basketball for four more years, but all of his college costs—tuition, books, food, and dormitory room—would be paid for by the university. In essence, Brooks would be able to gain a free college education, as long as he played basketball for the school.

But then again, it was baseball not basket-

*Frank Broyles (far right), Athletic Director of the University of Arkansas, is shown here with Brooks and his parents in 1976 when Robinson was inducted into the Arkansas Sports Hall of Fame.*

*Paul Richards took over as Orioles manager in 1955 and was their manager for seven seasons.*

ball that Brooks had hoped to make his career. Brooks knew that he had aroused considerable interest from some of the local baseball scouts who worked for major-league teams. Now that he had graduated from high school, some of these scouts would be coming around to offer him a professional contract. Which team would he choose to join?

One scout, a man named Lindsay Deal, was an old friend of Brooks's father. A former ball-player himself, Deal did some scouting for the Baltimore Orioles. Months before Brooks graduated, Deal had sent a letter to Paul Richards, the general manager and field manager with the Orioles. The letter read:

Dear Paul:

I am writing you in regard to a kid named Brooks Robinson. I think he measures up to having a chance in major league baseball.

I think he is a natural third baseman although he has been playing both second and third.

He will be 18 years old May 18 and graduates from Little Rock Senior High School on May 27. He is 6-feet 1-inch in height and weighs 175. His physique is outstanding for a boy this age. He bats right and throws right.

He is no speed demon but neither is he a truck horse. I believe in a year or two he will be above average in speed.

He hit well over .400 last year in American Legion baseball, including all tournament games. At tournament in Altus, Oklahoma, he was awarded the trophy for being the outstanding player.

Brooks has a lot of power, baseball savvy and is always cool when the chips are down. This boy is the best prospect I've seen since Billy Goodman came to Atlanta to play when I was playing there. That is the reason I am contacting you.

I thought you might be interested in him and able to make as good an offer as anyone else. Otherwise, I wouldn't have bothered you with it.

This boy can go to most any university in the Southwest on a scholarship and will do so if he doesn't receive a contract in major league baseball. I know his parents well; in fact, we attend the same church.

He has been bird-dogged [scouted] by scouts for the past three years. Here are some of the clubs I know are definitely interested: Patterson of the Phillies; Camp and McHale of Detroit; Donald of the Yankees; Jonnard of the Giants, now with Kansas City; Rice of the Red Sox; Hahn of the Cardinals, and a scout from the White Sox. I've forgotten his name but he lives in Oklahoma. You probably know who I am talking about.

Hope this finds you and your family in good health. Best wishes for a successful season.

Sincerely,
Lindsay Deal

Paul Richards read the letter and sent it on to his director of scouting for Baltimore. Sure enough, Brooks had already received lots of interest from lots of teams—at final count, twelve of the sixteen major-league clubs then in existence had come to see Brooks play and liked what they saw.

Right after graduation, Brooks and his parents sat down to discuss his options. First off, Brooks decided that as much as he loved basketball and the idea of receiving a college scholarship, he loved baseball even more. Only by signing a professional baseball contract could he make his childhood dream come true.

Brooks decided he was going to play base-ball—if one of those twelve teams offered him a contract. As it turned out, they all did. The scouts came to his home in Pulaski Heights, and each one tried to convince Brooks that his organization was the best place to play. In those days, the annual free agent draft did not yet exist. As a result, scouts from each team could go after anybody they wanted, so long as the player was not already under contract to some other club.

The teams that expressed the greatest interest in Brooks were the New York Giants, the Detroit Tigers, the Cincinnati Reds, and the Orioles. There was lots of talk about Brooks's chances for making the majors and, of course, signing a contract and receiving a signing bonus. It was all very exciting for the young high school graduate.

By May 29, 1955, two teams were left in the chase—Cincinnati and Baltimore. Brooks invited each team's scout to his home for one last discussion. That night, Brooks carefully considered the two offers. The next day, he first called Paul Florence, who was the scout for the Reds. After thanking Florence for all his kindness and interest, Brooks announced that he had decided to sign with the Orioles.

The next call went to Art Ehlers, the Baltimore scout. The Orioles had offered Brooks a bonus of $4,000, a decent sum in those days, to sign with their club. But Ehlers made it quite clear that there was no guaranteeing Brooks's future as a major-leaguer.

"Our scouts have rated Brooks above average," Ehlers told the Robinson family. "We know he can field. We know he has the physical tools, too. And he has the right attitude. The question really is his hitting. Can he hit big-league pitching? The scouts gave him a C [average] rating in speed and about the same on his arm, but I can name you lots of players in the big leagues who were rated the same when they signed.

"So we want to farm Brooks out and see what he's got. If he shows ability in the minors, you can be sure we'll bring him up and in a hurry. Baltimore, as you know, is building a team. Young players with talent will be playing major-league ball with us quicker than with older, more established clubs. If you've got it, you'll be with Baltimore before you know it, Brooks," the scout concluded.

And with those assurances ringing in his ears, Brooks Robinson signed the contract with Baltimore.

# 4

# WELCOME TO THE MINOR LEAGUES

The first stop on Brooks's way to the majors actually began at Memorial Stadium, the home of the Orioles in Baltimore. As soon as he signed his contract with the Birds, Brooks was flown to Baltimore to meet manager Paul Richards, one of the most respected men in baseball.

It was a long way from Little Rock to Baltimore. When he got to town, the 18-year-old Brooks spent the night at the Southern Hotel. Most of the next day he wandered around downtown Baltimore, looking at all the sights and buildings. That evening, Brooks hopped into a taxi and, as nonchalantly as possible, told the cabbie, "Memorial Stadium, please."

It was all a brand-new experience for the teenager, one that he would never forget. Upon arriving at the stadium, Brooks was met by Art Ehlers, the scout who had signed him, and introduced to the team's manager.

"I've seen you play a few times," Richards informed his new recruit, "and I've liked what I've seen. I want you to stay with us for a few

*Robinson receives encouragement in 1955 from veteran Willie Miranda, the first of a string of slick-fielding shortstops who played alongside Brooks.*

27

days. Get acquainted. We are going to Cleveland tomorrow and you can go along on the trip. After that, we'll be sending you to our affiliate in York, Pennsylvania. It's Class B (which corresponds to the current Class AA level) in the Piedmont League. You'll get plenty of opportunity. Now, go get fixed up with a uniform. You can take batting practice after the regulars have had their licks."

Needless to say, Brooks was walking on air. Not only had he just signed a professional baseball contract and received a big bonus, but here he was at Memorial Stadium, chatting with the great Paul Richards. Best of all, Brooks was allowed to suit up with the Orioles before joining them on a road trip to Cleveland.

The road trip to Cleveland was another dream come true. But then, after all the excitement of seeing the big leagues, it was time for getting down to business—and down to the minors. Dispatched to the York White Roses, Robinson was assigned to play second base. He quickly made himself comfortable there, and his first pro season got off to a fine start.

Away from home for the first time, Robinson was having a ball off the field, too. He and his teammate Gene Oden shared a rented room in a private home in York. On long, hot summer nights, the two young ballplayers would try to beat the heat by driving over to the local YMCA. There, they would climb the fence and take a late-night swim in the Y's pool.

Life in the minors can be great fun at times, but it is usually remembered by most major league players as consisting of long bus rides, poorly lit fields, crummy food, and more than a touch of homesickness. That is no accident; baseball life in the minors is *supposed* to be

*Memorial Stadium in the mid-1950s, when Brooks Robinson was a young player. The trees and grass in back of the center-field scoreboard were replaced by bleacher seats in 1961.*

relatively uncomfortable; otherwise, there would be little incentive to climb out of the minors and play in the Big Show. Minor league baseball is meant to test not only your physical skills, but also your mental dedication to the game. How much are you willing to sacrifice to get to the big leagues? For a lucky few, like Brooks Robinson, they succeed—and their boyhood dreams come true by being promoted to the majors.

Brooks had a terrific 1955 season in York, and wound up with .331 average and 11 home runs. But the real high point came during an exhibition game. The Orioles had come to town to play the Class B club, and the York White Roses surprised the big leaguers with a big 13-1 victory. And 3 of those runs came off a first-inning homer by Brooks Robinson.

As soon as the minor-league season ended, Robinson was told to report to Baltimore. The major-league season would go on for seven more weeks. Robinson arrived in the morning and decided to go straight to Memorial Stadium, because the Orioles had an afternoon game with

*Brooks Robinson's 1957 Topps bubble gum card.*

the Washington Senators. He arrived early, got suited up and worked out, and then as game-time approached, he found a place on the bench to sit back and watch the action.

Minutes later, however, Robinson found himself right in the middle of the action. One of the Baltimore coaches suddenly rushed up to him and yelled, "Hey, Robbie. Leppert [the regular third baseman] isn't feeling well. You start at third."

It took a few innings before Robinson could actually believe that he was playing in his first major-league game. In his first at-bat he grounded out, but on his second try, he whistled a line drive past third for a base hit. And later on he collected another single, this one good for his first run batted in.

The Birds won the game 3-1, with young Brooks Robinson going 2-for-4. As soon as it was over, Robinson raced to the telephone to tell his family the good news. The Robinsons could not have been happier, and Brooks in particular was excited after making the big jump from class-B ball to the major leagues. But the young ballplayer was in for a rude shock. After the heroics of that first game, he went 0-for-18 with 10 strikeouts in his next five appearances. "That opened my eyes," Brooks admitted. "I knew from then on I was going to have to work like blazes."

When the 1955 season finally came to an end, Brooks knew in his heart that he would most likely spend the next season back down in the minors. He would have to improve his hitting and gain more skill at hitting the curve ball and laying off the bad pitches. But he also knew that he had spent a little time in the majors and had enjoyed himself. So much so that he could not wait to get back to Baltimore.

Robinson spent the winter playing ball in Colombia, South America, and then in the spring of '56 he was assigned to play at San Antonio in the AA Texas League. He had an exceptional year there, but the season was interrupted when he injured his right knee sliding into second base. Something popped in the joint, and it turned out to be a torn cartilage.

Some serious thought was given to operating on the knee. But back in the 1950s, arthroscopic surgery had yet to be invented and conventional knee-surgery was considered a risky business. Luckily, the swelling finally went down by itself and Robinson returned to the San Antonio lineup.

Despite the injury, he finished with a .272 average and 74 RBI's, and led the league in putouts and fielding average at third base. At the end of the minor-league season, he was once again called up to the majors, this time for fifteen games. Although he batted only .227 during that stint, included in those hits was his first big-league homer.

Robinson was encouraged by his first two pro ball seasons. He knew it was only a matter of time before he would graduate from the minors and make the major-league club permanently.

# 5

# MAKING THE GRADE

After an excellent spring training in 1957, Brooks Robinson officially became a member of the Baltimore Orioles. Veteran third baseman George Kell, whom the Orioles had acquired early in the 1956 season, was moved to first base and the 20 year-old rookie took over at third.

But only two weeks later, in a game against the Washington Senators, disaster struck. After taking a lead off first base, Robinson dove back into the bag to avoid a pickoff throw. In the process, his right knee locked and he ripped the same piece of cartilage he had injured the year before while playing in San Antonio.

This time, however, the cartilage was completely torn in half, and surgery was necessary. And while the operation was considered a success, it knocked Robinson out of action for more than two months. When the doctors finally gave him the go-ahead to play, he was once again sent down to the minors. He ended up spending thirty days in San Antonio before being called back to the big club.

*Brooks retrieves a wild pickoff throw during a 1957 spring training game. But, as in 1956, he spent most of the season with San Antonio.*

But by then it was late July, and Robinson never really did reach his peak form. In that injury-shortened season, he hit a disappointing .239 in only 50 games.

Robinson knew all along that the game of baseball—especially professional baseball—was a most difficult occupation. Not only was it very competitive, but at any time an unexpected injury could knock even the best of players out of action.

As he slowly recuperated from his knee surgery, Robinson worried that he was losing valuable time in his quest to become a regular starter on the major-league club. But instead of feeling sorry for himself, the young third base-man determined that the spring of 1958 would be his time to nail down the starting job.

At spring training camp, Robinson went after the position with great enthusiasm. His hard work paid off, and by Opening Day he was the Orioles starting third baseman. In fact, Robinson played 145 games in '58 (in those days, the season was only 154 games); and even though he was a bit disappointed with his batting statistics—a .238 average with 3 home runs—he was happy to have finally won the job.

Robinson had already proven himself an excellent defenseman, and he knew it was only a matter of time until his offensive output improved. Yet once again, fate intervened. It seemed that Robinson would never fulfill his potential as a major leaguer.

This time, though, it was not an injury that took him out of the lineup—it was military duty. Before the 1959 season began, he was called upon to serve six months in the National Guard at Fort Hood. In the 1950s, military service was

*In 1957, veteran third baseman George Kell was very helpful to his eventual successor and fellow Arkansan, Brooks Robinson.*

compulsory for every able-bodied young man, and Robinson had volunteered for the Guard rather than wait to be drafted into the Army for what would likely be a two-year hitch.

By the time his six-month stint was up, Robinson was in excellent physical shape, but he had missed a large portion of spring training. During that time, a shortstop named Billy Klaus had been moved to third base and had played the position well. Robinson did his best to win back his old job, but his timing was off and even his best was not quite good enough.

About a month into the '59 season, Robinson was summoned to manager Paul Richards' office. And even though he had feared the worst, Robinson could not stop the tears from welling up in his eyes when Richards told him the bad news: he was once again being shipped to the minor leagues—this time to Vancouver.

Brooks relates the story in his autobiography *Putting It All Together.* "Brooks," the manager said, "you need work, and out there [in Vancouver, Canada] you can play every day. Go out there and play yourself into shape. If you get your game together, I'll bring you back to Baltimore at the All-Star break."

It may have been the most devastating blow in Robinson's young career. But, fortunately, on the long airplane flight to Vancouver, he had plenty of time to let his disappointment play itself out. By the time he reached his minor-league destination, Brooks Robinson had resolved to play the best ball of his career and work his way back to the big leagues just as soon as possible.

Sure enough, when the All-Star break came around, Robinson was hitting at a .331 clip. True to his word, Paul Richards brought the youngster back from the minors—this time for good. Over the next eighteen years, Brooks Robinson would be a permanent fixture at third base for the Baltimore Orioles.

*Brooks poses in his Vancouver uniform after his 1959 demotion to the minors.*

That summer of 1959 was the start of something else for the 22-year-old from Arkansas. Shortly after he had been recalled from Vancouver, Robinson flew to Boston with the Orioles. During the trip he was smitten by a young flight attendant. It took him about an hour to get his courage up, but the shy young ballplayer finally started a conversation with her.

After the plane landed in Boston, Robinson asked the attendant—her name was Constance Butcher—to have dinner with him. She agreed, and a year and a half later, Brooks and Constance were married in her hometown of Windsor, Ontario, Canada.

The year 1959 had indeed proven to be a turning point for Brooks Robinson, both on and off the field. And even better years were ahead.

# 6

# AN ALL-TIME ALL-STAR

From 1960, until his retirement in 1977, Robinson steadily rose to the top of his profession. And by the time he was ready to hang up his spikes, most baseball fans and experts were in perfect agreement: Brooks Robinson was very likely the best fielding third baseman ever to have played in the American League. Casey Stengel, whose career as a player and manager stretched from 1912 to the 1960s, observed, "Traynor was the best, but Robinson is nearly up there with him."

Pie Traynor, the Hall of Fame third baseman, said about Brooks, "he had exceptional reflexes and the strongest pull hitters couldn't get the ball by him." Most American League hitters would agree.

Those years also marked an overall improvement in the Baltimore Orioles as a team. During the 1950s, under the guidance of Paul Richards, the Orioles were in the process of trying to replace their older starters with younger players. That meant some difficult years of transition for the team, but by 1960 things were

*For his outstanding play in 1964, Brooks is presented with the Ty Cobb Memorial Award by announcer Mel Allen.*

clearly coming together in Baltimore. And Brooks Robinson was a major piece of the "glue" that held the club together.

In fact, in 1960, the Orioles almost flew off with the pennant. The New York Yankees were perennial contenders during these years, but when the Bronx Bombers came to Baltimore for a three-game series in September, they were only one slim game ahead of the Orioles in the standings.

The Orioles won three straight games from New York, thrusting Baltimore into first place in the American League. But alas, just one week later Baltimore visited New York, and there the Yankees returned the favor by winning four straight from their rivals. That put the Yanks back in the driver's seat, and that is where they stayed for the rest of the season.

Still, it had been a good year for Brooks Robinson and the Orioles. The Birds had challenged the Yankees all the way, leaving the strong feeling among baseball people that the Orioles were an up-and-coming team. Robinson had finally established himself, both as a hitter and a fielder. He batted .294 in 1960, with 14 home runs and 88 RBIs. And he collected more putouts and assists than any other third baseman in the league.

Over the next few seasons, the team continued to battle for the American League pennant. But while the Orioles consistently played well, they always seemed to fall just short. Robinson, however, kept getting better and better. Year after year his hitting hovered around the .300 mark, and his home runs and RBI totals remained notably high.

Even more impressive was his outstanding

work in the field. Brooks Robinson did not just make the routine plays at third base; he had a knack for making the spectacular ones, too. It was well known—and Robinson was the first to admit it—that he was not particularly fast afoot; nor was he blessed with a great throwing arm. Nevertheless, he made up for those apparent deficiencies with amazing quickness, reacting almost automatically to a hard-hit ball and firing it off just as fast as he had gloved it.

Things really came together in 1964, when Robinson made one slight adjustment in spring training. Always a reliable hitter, he had been using a relatively light bat throughout his career—one that weighed only 31 ounces. But that year an Oriole coach suggested he try a bat that weighed 33 ounces and was an inch longer than his regular bat.

Robinson knew this was highly irregular. Most players tended to start off with bats that were too heavy for them, only to switch to a lighter weight. But here he was, going to a heavier, longer bat. The result? In 1964, Brooks Robinson had his best year yet, hitting .317 with 28 homers and 118 RBIs. Those offensive stats along with his always awesome defensive play earned him the American League Most Valuable Player award.

Robinson, of course, was thrilled with the honor. But happy as he was for himself, the 1964 MVP still was not satisfied. The Orioles finished third in 1964, the same spot they would finish in 1965. But Robinson was not about to give up. Playing in a World Series had long been a dream of his. And like Brooks Robinson's other dreams, this too would soon become a reality.

# 7

# ROBINSON AND ROBINSON

Before the next season even began, Baltimore greatly improved its chances for a world championship. Eager to improve their offensive punch, the Orioles traded several players to land Frank Robinson, a super-slugging outfielder with the Cincinnati Reds. Frank had been named the National League MVP in 1960, and now, at the age of 30 (one year older than Brooks), he still swung a big bat.

Both Robinsons had great 1966 seasons: Frank hit .316, with 49 home runs and 122 RBIs, while Brooks averaged .269, smacking 23 homers and 100 RBIs. The Orioles were so good that they simply ran away from the rest of the competition, winning the American League pennant by nine games over the second-place Minnesota Twins. The once-mighty Yankees wound up last in the league—26½ games behind, a position they had not finished in since 1912.

*Brooks scores the first run on a wild pitch in the 1966 All-Star game as Sandy Koufax covers the plate. Koufax was the starter against the Orioles in game 2 of the World Series that year.*

The Baltimore Orioles would meet the Los Angeles Dodgers in the World Series. The National League's Dodgers featured a great pitching staff, led by the hard-throwing combination of Don Drysdale and Sandy Koufax. Koufax was the lone Cy Young winner in 1965 and, in a unanimous vote, again in 1966; until 1967 there was not a Cy Young award for each league. Many baseball fans thought they were simply too good for the Orioles in a short series where pitching so often dominates. But the Orioles had Brooks Robinson plus Frank Robinson. Frank led the American League in hitting, RBI's and homers and easily won the Most Valuable Player award, the first player to ever win the coveted honor in both leagues. The runners-up in the award voting were his teammates Brooks Robinson and Boog Powell.

The first game went to the Orioles as Brooks and Frank hit back-to-back home runs in the first inning against Drysdale. Jim Palmer shutout the Dodgers in the second game as the O's won 6-0. Games 3 and 4 showed that the Dodgers did indeed have great pitching; in each game the Orioles managed just one run, but that

*Robinson leaped for joy when the last out was recorded in game 4 of the 1966 Series. This picture of the Orioles celebrating was named the sports photo of the year.*

was more than the Dodgers could score. The only two runs the Dodgers scored in the series were in game 1 as they managed to hit just .142 for the four games against the Orioles.

When the final out was recorded, joyous celebrations rocked the city of Baltimore. It was a glorious time, and Brooks Robinson was especially thrilled that his team won—thrilled, except for one thing. While it was truly terrific that the O's had won it all, Brooks was a little disappointed with his own contribution to the World Series victory. Overall, he had batted only .214, with 3 hits in 14 at-bats. He had performed well in the field; but in his heart he knew he had not really played his best.

Keep in mind that in 1966, Brooks Robinson's best was really something. The fans—and Robinson himself—had come to expect a lot from the versatile third baseman. And with good reason. Robinson had been named to the American League All-Star team every year since 1960, and that streak would continue right through 1974. Perhaps his greatest All Star performance came in the 1966 game, where he was named MVP after wracking up 3 hits, including a home run, and handling 8 chances in the field without an error. A perennial All-Star, Robinson would compile a lifetime batting average of .289 (13-for-45) in 18 appearances and handle 43 error-free plays at third.

It was that standard of performance Robinson wanted dearly to match the next time the Orioles made it to the World Series. As it developed, he did not get his chance until 1969. And that Series—the ill-fated meeting with the New York Mets—was hardly worth waiting for. Robinson's embarrassing .053 hitting made it seem more like a nightmare than a dream.

When the 1967 season started, the defending World Champions were confident that they could repeat. Not only did they have a veteran team, their minor-league system was producing a number of young birds that would make the Orioles contenders for a long time. But the Red Sox, led by MVP Carl Yaztrzemski and Cy Young Award winner Jim Lonborg, won the American League pennant. The Orioles pitching was paced by rookie Tom Phoebus, who won 14 games. But the rest of the staff produced not even one 10-game winner and the Orioles slumped to sixth place.

Midway through the 1968 season, manager Hank Bauer was replaced by fiery Earl Weaver, who would guide the team through the 1970s. The Orioles rebounded in 1968 to win 91 games only to finish in second place behind the Tigers. But in 1969, Orioles were determined; they compiled a 19-5 record in the spring and then ran away with from the rest of the league during the regular season, winning 109 games and finishing 19 games ahead of the Tigers. Brooks had a sub-par year at the plate hitting just .234, but he again led the league's third basemen in fielding. It was the seventh time in the past eight years that he was tops at his position.

The year 1969 was a year of change in the majors as expansion teams were added in Montreal and San Diego in the National League, and in Seattle and Kansas City in the American League. [The Royals replaced the Athletics who had departed Kansas City for Oakland]. For the first time the leagues were divided into divisions, East and West, and the winners of each had to play each other for the right to go on to the World

*The brilliant and combative manager Earl Weaver took over the Orioles in 1968. To get closer to umpires when he argued with them, Weaver would often turn his cap around. In his 17 years as manager, he was ejected from almost 100 games.*

Series. The Orioles faced the Twins and swept them in three games as Brooks hit .500. The team was confident as it went into the series against the "Amazin' Mets," surprise winners in the National League.

Everyone predicted the Orioles would win easily, and they did in the first game, scoring a 4-1 victory over Tom Seaver. But that was it for the O's; the Mets won the next four games as the Orioles were held to a team batting average of .142 against the inspired New Yorkers. Led by Koosman and Seaver on the mound, and Donn Clendenon and Ron Swoboda at bat, the Mets were too much. Swoboda also made two sensational catches in the field, one of which robbed Brooks of a sure triple in the fourth game.

Although Brooks got an RBI on the play, one of two he had in the series, he had just 1 hit in 19 at-bats. Disappointed but undaunted, Brooks Robinson was more determined than ever to prove himself in the World Series.

When the 1970 season ended, the Orioles had again won the Eastern Championship with little competition, finishing 15 games ahead of the Yankees. They went into the AL Championships with three 20-game winners, Jim Palmer, Mike Cuellar, and Dave McNally. Brooks had a fine year, knocking in 94 runs, second on the team to big Boog Powell's 114 RBI's. Again the Orioles faced the Twins, and once again, they swept them in 3 games. Brooks hit .538 against the Minnesota pitching and eagerly looked forward to facing the National League winners, the Cincinnati Reds. He wanted to atone for his poor showing in the World Series the previous year.

And after that first error in game 1, he did just that—with an amazing display of fielding that has not been duplicated to this day. In the sixth inning, Cincinnati's Lee May hit a scorcher down the third-base line. It looked to be a sure double, but Robinson went far to his right, made a backhanded stab, and fired an off-balance throw that was just good enough to nip May at first base. It was the kind of play that even the Cincinnati fans could not help applauding.

Baltimore ended up winning both the first and second games of the 1970 Series as Robinson's defensive play continued to sparkle. Then in game 3, which was played in Baltimore, Cincinnati threatened to take an early lead in the first inning. With Reds on first and second and no one out, Tony Perez smashed the ball toward third. Robinson grabbed it and stepped on third base for out number one before hurling the ball to first to complete the double play. Then, just to make sure the threat was over, he snared Johnny Bench's line drive for the third out.

In the sixth inning, Brooks did it to Bench again. When the future Hall of Fame catcher blasted a rocket to Robinson's left, Robinson dove and snagged it in the air even as he was falling to the ground. He had robbed Bench of another sure hit.

By now it was apparent to all who were following the Series that Brooks Robinson was practically a one-man team. Not only was he a powerhouse at the plate (.429 with 2 home runs and 6 RBIs), but he was also taking the Big Red

*Brooks Robinson, described in the Orioles' media guide as "the most important and beloved Oriole of modern times," always took the time to give his autograph to fans.*

Machine apart defensively. The Reds managed to win the fourth game, but the Orioles were not to be denied as they won the Series, 4 games to 1. Brooks Robinson was named the MVP of the 1970 World Series. After the last game, a representative from the baseball Hall of Fame called upon Robinson. He requested that the Baltimore third baseman send his glove to the Hall. Robinson was more than happy to oblige.

The following year, the Orioles easily captured the American League East flag again, finishing 10 games ahead of the Tigers. This time they had four 20-game winners as Pat Dobson joined Palmer, Cuellar and McNally to give the Orioles an awesome starting staff. It is the only time since the Chicago White Sox of 1920 that one team had four 20-game winners in the same year. This time the Orioles' western opponents were the Oakland Athletics, but the result was the same; the Orioles swept in three games as Brooks hit .364. In the third game, A's manager Dick Williams ordered his pitcher to give Ellie Hendricks an intentional walk to load the bases and bring up Brooks Robinson. Brooks then laced a single to bring home two runs, the margin of victory for the Orioles.

The Orioles then faced the Pittsburgh Pirates in the Series. Once again, Brooks Robinson rose to the occasion. He had another spectacular Series, fielding flawlessly and hitting .318 with 5 RBIs. In game 2, Brooks tied a World Series record by reaching base five straight times on three hits and two walks. In the sixth game, which went into extra innings, Dave McNally pitched out of a bases-loaded jam to set up the Orioles chance in the bottom of the tenth. After singles by Rettenmund and Frank Robinson,

Brooks brought in the winning run with a sacrifice fly. The seventh game would decide it all.

But this time the National Leaguers prevailed. Although the Orioles hung in till the very end, Pittsburgh, after losing the first two games, finally eked out a 2-1 victory in the seventh and final game.

Baltimore easily won the East again in 1973 only to fall to a powerful Oakland team in the League Championship Series. Oakland won again in the West division in 1974, while the Orioles edged out the Yankees by two games in the East. But again it was the star-studded Oakland team heading for the World Series. Brooks managed just one hit in the 1974 series against Oakland, an opening-game two-run homer, the only game the Orioles won.

It would prove to be Brooks's last chance for another World Series ring as the Orioles would not win the American League Championship again until 1979.

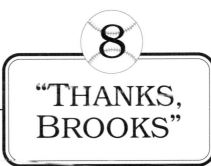

# 8

# "THANKS, BROOKS"

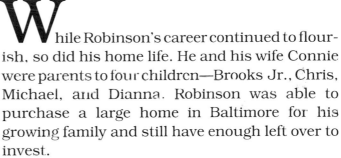

**W**hile Robinson's career continued to flourish, so did his home life. He and his wife Connie were parents to four children—Brooks Jr., Chris, Michael, and Dianna. Robinson was able to purchase a large home in Baltimore for his growing family and still have enough left over to invest.

Brooks Robinson had become a true local hero in the city of Baltimore. Not only did the fans admire his abilities on the field but they also loved him for his sportsmanship and dedication to the game. When he finally retired from active play in 1977, the Baltimore fans held a "Thanks, Brooks" Day to salute him. On September 18, a crowd of 51,798, the largest regular-season crowd in Baltimore history, came out to Memorial Stadium to pay tribute to Robinson and his family.

And then, to top it all off, the Baltimore management decided to retire his uniform

*Brooks owns every major fielding record for third basemen by a wide margin. He also holds the odd major-league record of hitting into the most triple plays with 4.*

number (5) in a ceremony that was conducted at the stadium on Opening Day 1978. What meant the most to Baltimore's fans was the fact that Robinson had played over 20 years in the big leagues, and every day of his major league career had been played for the Orioles.

By the time he left the lineup in 1977, the 40-year-old Brooks Robinson had collected a number of major-league records that attest to his defensive prowess. The most notable include the highest fielding percentage (in 100 or more games) by a third baseman (.971), most career chances (9,165), most career putouts (2,697), most career assists (6,205), and most career double plays (618).

And it was not only the numbers that proved Brooks's greatness; in the view of his major-league peers he was the best. In the book *Player's Choice*, 80 per cent of the major-league players polled picked Robinson as the top fielding third baseman of all time. No other player at any defensive position polled more than 20 percent.

Brooks Robinson had done it all in baseball, and had done it in spectacular fashion. In the summer of '83, he was elected to baseball's most select fraternity, the Hall of Fame in Cooperstown, New York.

Although Brooks Robinson's baseball career had reached its pinnacle when he was inducted into the Hall of Fame, Brooks's transition into baseball retirement was hardly a smooth one. Like the start of his major-league career, Brooks discovered that life outside baseball offered all sorts of challenges of its own, and that he had to face them with the same kind of guts and determination that he had shown in his playing career.

For starters, just about the time that Brooks was retiring from his role as an active player in 1977, he was looking forward to devoting all of his energies to managing his business investments, most notably, a sporting goods store that was located near Baltimore. But despite the best efforts of Brooks and his business partner, the sporting goods store suffered a decline in business and eventually went bankrupt. Brooks was saddled with a great amount of debt.

Brooks had to start paying people and the store's creditors out of his own life savings. But if there was one common thread throughout his life, it was the thread of never quitting. Brooks, above all, was a battler and competitor, and even though his plans of running a sporting goods store went sour, Brooks just did not give up. He gradually paid off all the money he owed, and then he went on to find other work to help take care of his family.

Today, more than twelve years later, Brooks has succeeded as much off the field as he did on the field. He overcame his first financial mistakes when he retired, and now Brooks is one of the busiest and most successful executives in the Baltimore area. His full-time job is with Crown Central Petroleum, an oil and gasoline company in Maryland. But in addition to his executive responsibilities with Crown, Brooks also finds time to work as a broadcaster on Orioles' baseball games, doing as many as 50 games a year. He has been doing this since 1977.

As you might imagine, Brooks Robinson is as loyal to his fans in Baltimore as they are to him. A good example of this is an incident that occured in 1974 when a Yale University sopho-

*Yale sophomore Stephanie Vardavas in 1974 wearing Brooks's uniform which he loaned her for Halloween. Her faculty adviser at Yale University was Bart Giamatti, who later became commissioner of baseball.*

more, Stephanie Vardavas, wrote to Brooks and asked him if she could borrow his uniform for Halloween. A week or two later, to her great surprise, she received a handwritten letter from Robinson. In it Brooks said that it was fine with him. However, the uniform belonged to the Orioles and that she should contact them, which she did. Because of Brooks's approval, she received a package in the mail with the uniform, cap, socks, and stirrups. She knew it was the real uniform because there was a button missing and the leg was worn from sliding. When Halloween came Stephanie put the uniform on for the first time. It was a big thrill.

Several years later Stephanie met Robinson at Memorial Stadium and he signed the photograph of her wearing his uniform. As she said, "Maybe someday I'll be the answer to a trivia

question: 'who's the only other person to wear number five for the Orioles?'"

Baseball fans everywhere will tell you that the only way to get into the Hall of Fame is to get a lot of hits and hit a lot of home runs. But for baseball fans who have followed Brooks Robinson's career for over 30 years, they will also tell you that there are a few very special Hall of Famers—people like Brooks Robinson—who deserve to be in a special Hall of Fame all by themselves.

*Brooks Robinson (far right) and George Kell (far left), inducted into the baseball Hall of Fame together in 1983, share a Texas League game that year with fellow Hall of Famers from Arkansas, Bill Dickey (middle left) and Travis Jackson (middle right). The plaques are from the Arkansas Sports Hall of Fame.*

# CHRONOLOGY

| | |
|---|---|
| May 18, 1937 | Brooks Calbert Robinson is born in Little Rock, Arkansas. |
| Spring, 1948 | Starts playing in Little Rock Midget League, playing both infield and pitching. Team wins Little Rock championship. |
| Spring, 1949 | Same team goes wins Arkansas Midget League State champion ship. |
| 1951-1954 | Plays for local Little Rock American Legion team. Ball club wins the state championship three out of four years. |
| May 27, 1955 | Graduates from Little Rock High School. |
| June 1, 1955 | Robinson signs with the Baltimore Orioles for a bonus of $4,000. |
| Spring, 1958 | After three years of injuries and false starts, Robinson claims the Orioles' third base spot. |
| Oct. 8, 1960 | Marries Constance Butcher. |
| Oct. 1964 | Named American League Most Valuable Player. |
| July 12, 1966 | Named All-Star game MVP with three hits including a home run. |
| 1966 | With teammate Frank Robinson, leads the Orioles to the American League pennant. |
| Oct. 6, 1969 | Hits an even .500 (7-14) in the League Championship Series over the Minnesota Twins. The Birds lose to the Miracle Mets in the World Series. |
| Oct. 15, 1970 | Hits .429, 2 HR, and 6 RBIs in the World Series, and is named Series Most Valuable Player. |
| July 23, 1974 | Plays in his last All-Star game after having been named to the squad for 15 years in a row. |
| 1976 | Inducted into the Arkansas Sports Hall of Fame. |
| Sept. 18, 1977 | Baltimore fans stage "Thanks, Brooks" Day at Memorial Stadium. 51,798 fans attend the game. |
| July, 1983 | Inducted into the Baseball Hall of Fame, Cooperstown, NY. |

**BROOKS CALBERT ROBINSON, JR.**
BALTIMORE A.L. 1955-1977
ESTABLISHED MODERN STANDARD OF EXCELLENCE
FOR THIRD BASEMEN, SETTING MAJOR LEAGUE
RECORDS AT HIS POSITION FOR SEASONS (23),
FIELDING PCT. (.971), GAMES (2,870), PUTOUTS
(2,697), ASSISTS (6,205), AND DOUBLE PLAYS (618).
HIT 268 CAREER HOME RUNS. NAMED TO 18
CONSECUTIVE ALL STAR TEAMS. MVP OF 1970
WORLD SERIES. AMERICAN LEAGUE MVP IN 1964.

# MAJOR LEAGUE STATISTICS

## BALTIMORE ORIOLES

| YEAR | TEAM | G | AB | R | H | 2B | 3B | HR | RBI | BA | SB |
|------|------|---|-----|---|---|----|----|----|-----|----|----|
| 1955 | Bal A | 6 | 22 | 0 | 2 | 0 | 0 | 0 | 1 | .091 | 0 |
| 1956 | | 15 | 44 | 5 | 10 | 4 | 0 | 1 | 1 | .227 | 0 |
| 1957 | | 50 | 117 | 13 | 28 | 6 | 1 | 2 | 14 | .239 | 1 |
| 1958 | | 145 | 463 | 31 | 110 | 16 | 3 | 3 | 32 | .238 | 1 |
| 1959 | | 88 | 313 | 29 | 89 | 15 | 2 | 4 | 24 | .284 | 2 |
| 1960 | | 152 | 595 | 74 | 175 | 27 | 9 | 14 | 88 | .294 | 2 |
| 1961 | | 163 | 668 | 89 | 912 | 38 | 7 | 7 | 61 | .287 | 1 |
| 1962 | | 162 | 634 | 77 | 192 | 29 | 9 | 23 | 86 | .303 | 3 |
| 1963 | | 161 | 589 | 67 | 148 | 26 | 4 | 11 | 67 | .251 | 2 |
| 1964 | | 163 | 612 | 82 | 194 | 35 | 3 | 28 | 118 | .317 | 1 |
| 1965 | | 144 | 559 | 81 | 166 | 25 | 2 | 18 | 80 | .297 | 3 |
| 1966 | | 157 | 620 | 91 | 167 | 35 | 2 | 23 | 100 | .269 | 2 |
| 1967 | | 158 | 610 | 88 | 164 | 25 | 5 | 22 | 77 | .269 | 1 |
| 1968 | | 162 | 608 | 65 | 154 | 36 | 6 | 17 | 75 | .253 | 1 |
| 1969 | | 156 | 598 | 73 | 140 | 21 | 3 | 23 | 84 | .234 | 2 |
| 1970 | | 158 | 608 | 84 | 168 | 31 | 4 | 18 | 94 | .276 | 1 |
| 1971 | | 156 | 589 | 67 | 160 | 21 | 1 | 20 | 92 | .272 | 0 |
| 1972 | | 153 | 556 | 48 | 139 | 23 | 2 | 8 | 64 | .250 | 1 |
| 1973 | | 155 | 549 | 53 | 141 | 17 | 2 | 9 | 72 | .257 | 2 |
| 1974 | | 153 | 553 | 46 | 159 | 27 | 0 | 7 | 59 | .288 | 2 |
| 1975 | | 144 | 482 | 50 | 97 | 15 | 1 | 6 | 53 | .201 | 0 |
| 1976 | | 71 | 218 | 16 | 46 | 8 | 2 | 3 | 11 | .211 | 0 |
| 1977 | | 24 | 47 | 3 | 7 | 2 | 0 | 1 | 4 | .149 | 0 |
| **Total** | | 2,896 | 10,654 | 1,232 | 2,848 | 482 | 68 | 268 | 1,357 | .267 | 28 |

| | | G | AB | R | H | 2B | 3B | HR | RBI | BA | SB |
|---|---|---|---|---|---|----|----|----|-----|----|----|
| **League Championship Series** (5 years) | | 18 | 69 | 9 | 24 | 6 | 0 | 2 | 7 | .348 | 0 |
| **World Series** (4 years) | | 21 | 76 | 9 | 20 | 2 | 0 | 3 | 14 | .263 | 0 |
| **All-Star Games** (15 years) | | 15 | 45 | 5 | 13 | 0 | 3 | 1 | 5 | .289 | 0 |

# FURTHER READING

Brown, Bob, *Baltimore Orioles 1989 Media Guide*. Baltimore, MD: 1989.

Burchard, Marshall and Sue Burchard, *Brooks Robinson: Sports Hero*. New York: Putnam, 1972.

Karst, Gene, and Martin J. Jones, Jr., *Who's Who in Professional Baseball*. New Rochelle, NY: Arlington House, 1973.

McCaffrey, Eugene and Roger McCaffrey, *Players' Choice*. New York: Facts on File, 1987.

Nelson, Kevin. *The Greatest Stories Ever Told About Baseball*. New York: Perigee, 1986.

Reichler, Joe, Ed. *The Baseball Encyclopedia, 8th ed.* New York: Macmillan, 1990.

Shatzkin, Mike and Jim Charlton, *The Ballplayers*. New York: Morrow, 1990.

Sporting News. *Official Baseball Guides, 1955-1977*. St. Louis, MO: The Sporting News, 1977.

Robinson, Brooks with Fred Bauer, *Putting It All Together*. New York: Hawthorn Books, 1971.

Robinson Brooks, with Jack Tobin. *Third Base is My Home*. Waco, TX: Word, 1974.

Zanger, Jack. *The Brooks Robinson Story*. New York: Julian Messner, 1967.

# INDEX

RICK WOLFF is the editorial director of sports books for Macmillan in New York City. A former professional player in the Detroit Tigers' minor league organization, Wolff has written several books about baseball, including *The Psychology of Winning Baseball* (Parker, 1986), *Breaking Into the Big Leagues* (Leisure, 1988) and *Baseball: A Laughing Matter* (The Sporting News, 1987). He also does on-air baseball analysis for ESPN, SportsChannel, and the Madison Square Garden Network.

JIM MURRAY, veteran sports columnist of the *Los Angeles Times*, is one of America's most acclaimed writers. He has been named "America's Best Sportswriter" by the National Association of Sportscasters and Sportswriters 14 times, was awarded the Red Smith Award, and was twice winner of the National Headliner Award. In addition, he was awarded the J. G. Taylor Spink Award in 1987 for "meritorious contributions to baseball writing." With this award came his 1988 induction into the National Baseball Hall of Fame in Cooperstown, New York. In 1990, Jim Murray was awarded the Pulitzer Prize for Commentary.

EARL WEAVER is the winningest manager in Baltimore Orioles history by a wide margin. He compiled 1,480 victories in his 17 years at the helm. After managing eight different minor league teams, he was given the chance to lead the Orioles in 1968. Under his leadership the Orioles finished lower than second place in the American League East only four times in 17 years. One of only 12 managers in big league history to have managed in four or more World Series, Earl was named Manager of the Year in 1979. The popular Weaver had his number 5 retired in 1982, joining Brooks Robinson, Frank Robinson, and Jim Palmer, whose numbers were retired previously. Earl Weaver continues his association with the professional baseball scene by writing, broadcasting, and coaching.